Chlori the Chloroplast is the first in a series of books in the

Sun Of Lex (SOL) Science Series

Copyright © 2021 Zachariyah Mercier

Cover design and illustrations by Zachariyah Mercier.

ISBN 978-1-8384911-0-9

Chlori the Chloroplast
Written and illustrated
By Zachariyah Mercier

SCIENCE SERIES

Chlori the Chloroplast

Think about the first time you ever opened a flower. It all just looked like flower gunk right? It all looked the same and it never really mattered right? Well you're wrong.
It all matters!

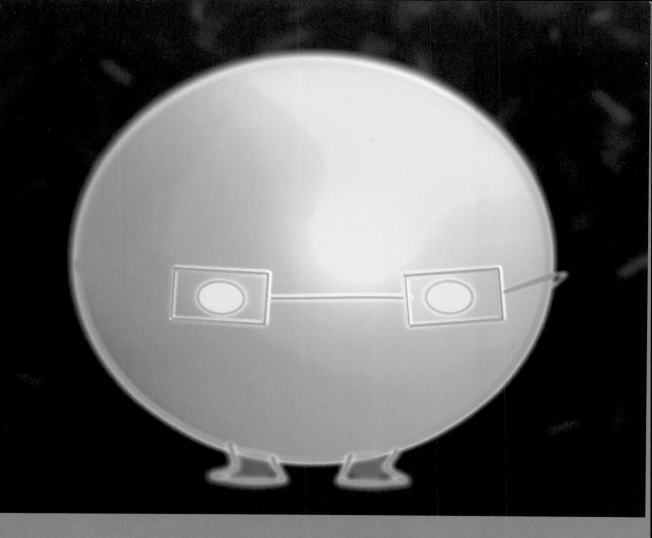

Meet Chlori.
Chlori is a chloroplast.
He lives in the plant cell. It's his family's
sworn duty to provide the grand flower
with its daily food. It's Chlori's birthright
to take the mantle of Chloro King when
his father passes on and a new flower is
created.

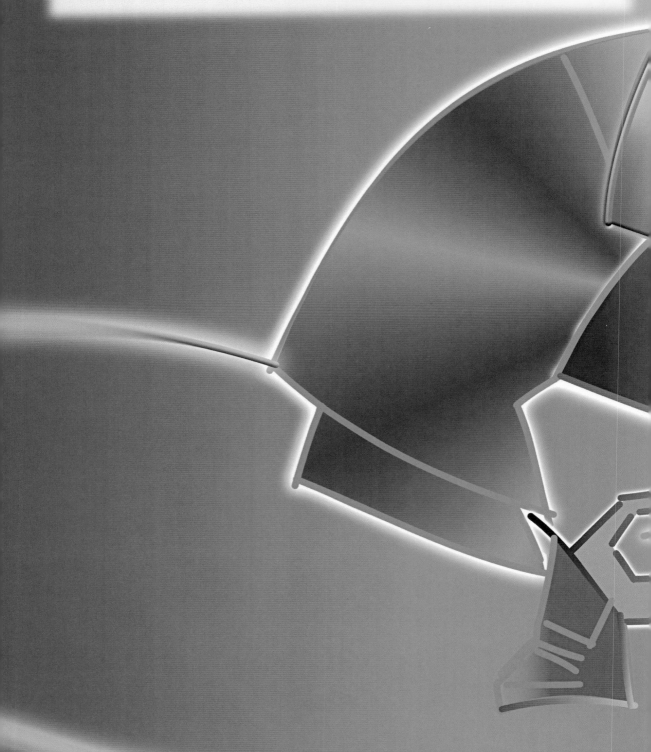

Chlori has always been terrified of becoming Chloro King and thinks he can't handle the pressure of such a huge role.

He knows if he fails not only will he tarnish the Chloroplast legacy for generations to come, the grand flower will eventually shrivel up and be no more.

One day Chlori ventured to the wisest being in the cell, Neo the nucleus.
He who had guided many others, offered wisdom to the young prodigy.

"My boy, your father had similar worries. He was terrified that he may tarnish Chloroplast legacy.
Your fears only display how determined and passionate you are about honouring your role.

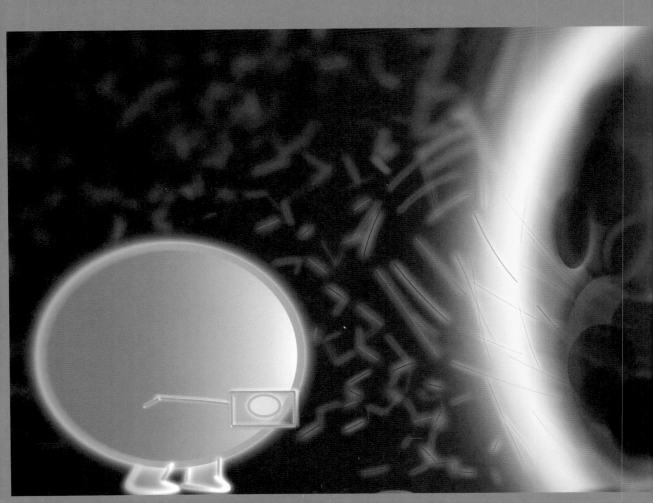

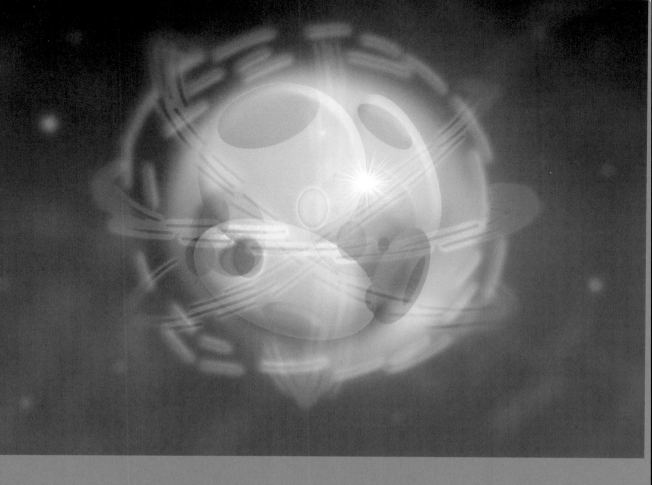

You carry chlorophyll that helps you to absorb the light energy.
Once you have that energy you turn it into the food for the cell, by converting it into sugars that can be used by our beloved cell.
But your job doesn't stop there.
Look up."

"What am I looking at?" Chlori asked.
"Can you see all those people running around and playing?"
Neo answered as he pointed into the distance. "Yes", replied Chlori inquisitively.

"Well my boy they are playing and breathing in fresh air because our grand flower has created oxygen, you will help to create oxygen.

You are an important part of a process we call Photosynthesis.
You're destined for greatness my son and greatness you will find."

Encouraged by this new knowledge,
Chlori was excited, to start his journey.
He trained his body to absorb maximum
energy.

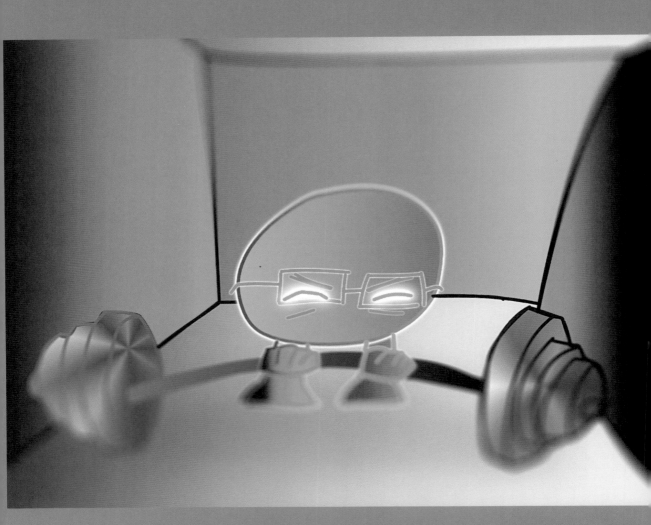

He studied the ways of those who
had come before him and worked hard
until he mastered his future role.

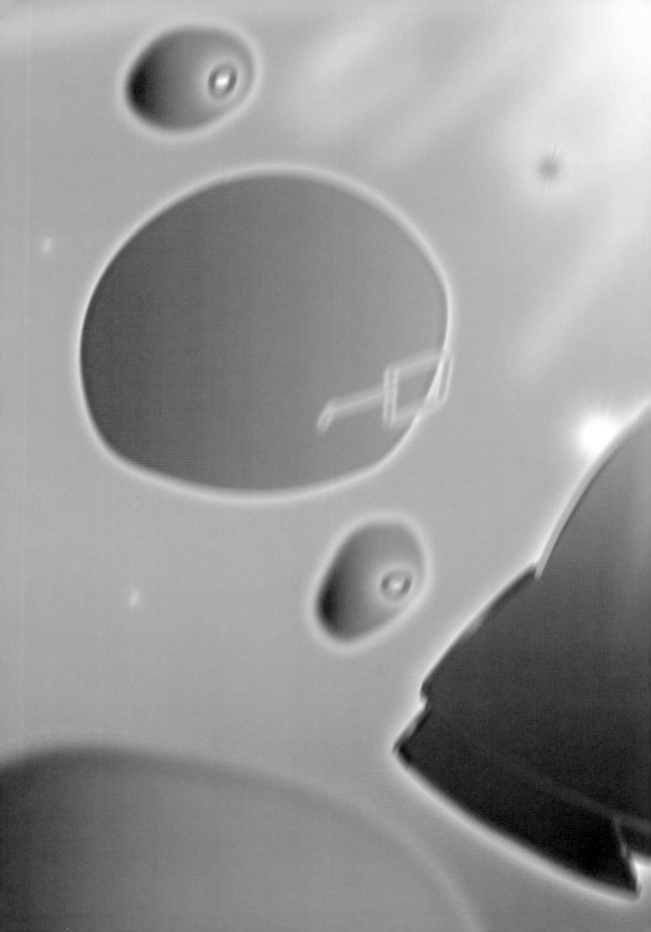

Chlori looked to his father for inspiration. His father had pushed him to the very limit and Chlori loved him for it.

However everybody knew a time would come when Chlori would have to take on the role of his father.

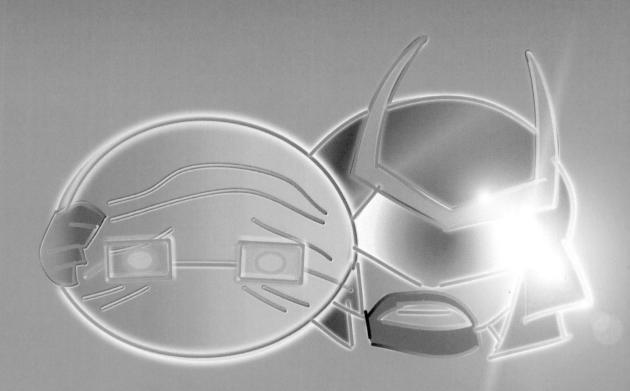

That time came sooner than Chlori imagined.
One day as Chlori was telling his father
about everything he had learned,
Chlori's father began to feel weak.

He told Chlori that it was his time to pass on.

Chlori felt scared and wanted to scream.
He wanted to break down but he couldn't.

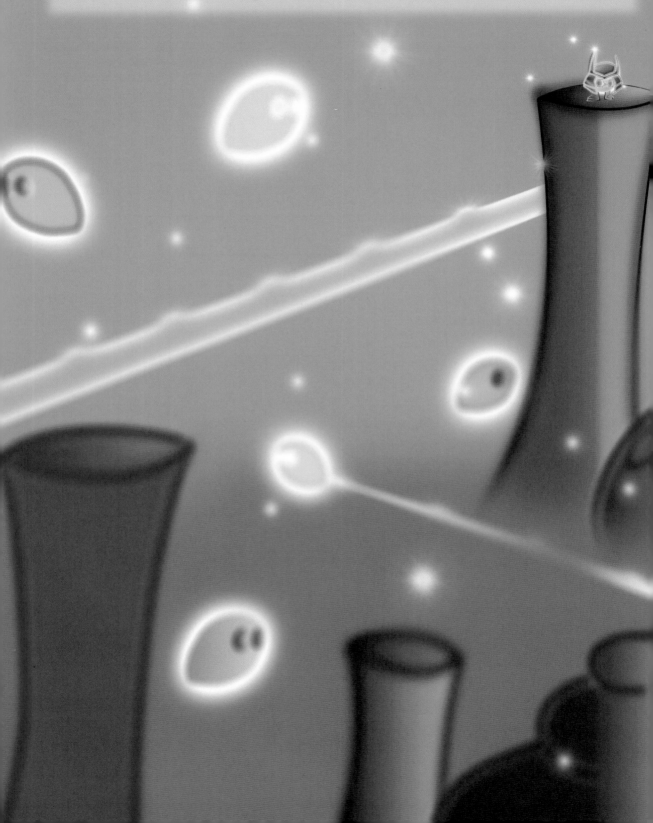

He knew exactly what he had to do and why.

He was the new Chloro King...

Now we have a new grand flower that blooms brighter than all the others.

Glossary

Plant Cell
Cells are considered the basic unit of Life.

Chlorophyll
Chlorophyll is the chemical in the Chloroplast that provides the energy needed to absorb the sun.

Chloroplast
Chloroplasts can be found inside the plant cell. They absorb the light and turn it into sugar which feeds the plant.
This process is called photosynthesis.

Nucleus
Nucleus is like the cell's brain. It helps control functions like reproduction and eating.

Oxygen
Plants create most of the oxygen we humans use through photosynthesis.